Library of Congress Catalog Card Number: 62-13951
Printed in the United States of America

B C D E

LET'S FIND OUT ABOUT

WINTER

by

MARTHA and CHARLES SHAPP

Pictures by László Roth

FRANKLIN WATTS, INC.
575 Lexington Avenue, New York 22

There are four seasons in the year –

spring,

summer,

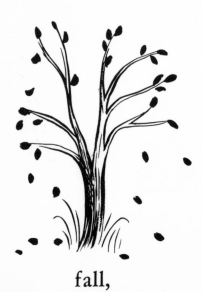

fall,

and winter.

Some like summer.

Some people like spring.

Others like the fall.

And some like winter best of all.

When is winter?
Winter is when it gets cold and you must wear
 your warmest clothing.

Winter is when it's so cold that your breath
comes out like steam.

In the winter the thermometer goes way down.

It's so cold that water freezes into ice.

It's fun to skate on the ice.

But it's not fun to slip and fall on the ice.

Winter is when the snow falls.

Everything looks nice in the snow.

You can have fun in the snow.

You can roll little balls of snow into big, big balls.

Look at snowflakes through a magnifying glass.
Every snowflake has six points.

Winter days are very short.

The first day of winter is the shortest day of the year.

Even the trees look cold in winter.
The leaves are all gone.

Only tiny, tiny buds are on the trees.
In the buds are the leaves that will come out in the spring.

There are some trees that stay green all winter.

They are called evergreens.

Some animals don't mind the winter cold.

Other animals don't like the winter cold.

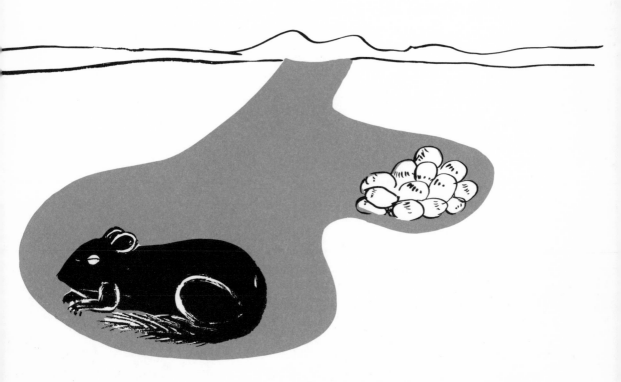

They sleep under the ground through the winter.

Some animals sleep through the winter in mud
under the water.

Some sleep under rocks.

People must keep warm in the winter.

Christmas comes in the winter.
Everybody likes Christmas.

There are four seasons in the year,

winter,

spring,

summer,

fall.

Don't you think that winter
is the best season of all?

VOCABULARY (100 words)

a
all
and
animals
are
at

balls
best
big
breath
buds
but

called
can
Christmas
clothing
cold
come(s)

day(s)
don't
down

even
evergreens
every
everybody
everything

fall(s)
first
four
freezes
fun

gets
glass
goes
gone

green
ground

has
have

ice
in
into
is
it('s)

keep

leaves
like(s)
little
look(s)

magnifying
mind
mud
must

nice
not

of
on
only
other(s)
out

people
points

rocks
roll

season(s)

short(est)
six
skate
sleep
slip
snow
snowflake(s)
so
some
spring
stay
steam
summer

that
the
there
thermometer
they
think
through
tiny
to
trees

under

very

warm(est)
water
way
wear
when
will
winter

year
you
your